ℛ ℒ . . .

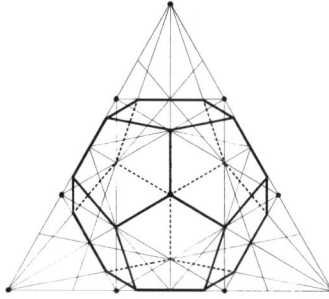

VIDYA

| Vol. XXV | Summer 2024 | Number 3 |

> THEOSOPHY, in its abstract meaning, is Divine Wisdom, or the aggregate of the knowledge and wisdom that underlie the Universe—the homogeneity of eternal GOOD; and in its concrete sense it is the sum total of the same as allotted to man by nature on this earth.
>
> H.P. BLAVATSKY

Vidya, or Knowledge, points to the timeless *Theosophia,* the source and synthesis of science, religion and philosophy. This publication is consecrated to the keynote sounded by the great Founders of the Theosophical Movement, who have appeared to all peoples, throughout all ages. As a journal of inquiry into the Teachings of Theosophy and its apt applications to daily life, VIDYA is offered to all who seek the path of spiritual self-regeneration in the service of humanity.

VIDYA
Volume XXV No. 3

Edited by students of the United Lodge of Theosophists, Santa Barbara

p. 194 sources: *A Survey of Buddhism*, ninth edition 2002 by Sangharakshita. *The Dhammapada with Udanavarga,* edited by R.N. Iyer and online DDSA (Digital Dictionary of South Asia).

* Requests for discount prices and other communications should be addressed to Editor, VIDYA, *1407 Chapala St., Santa Barbara, CA 93101, U.S.A. or sent to info@concordgrovepress.org.*

VIDYA *is a quarterly publication of Concord Grove Press on behalf of Universal Theosophy Fellowship. It is edited by associates of the United Lodge of Theosophists in Santa Barbara. In adherence to the U.L.T. principle of impersonality, all student contributions are anonymous; for the purposes of listing with Amazon Kindle Direct Publishing services, the author of this work is the pseudonymn "ULT Students".*

Donations and bequests in support of VIDYA *are tax-exempt and should be made directly to the Treasurer, Universal Theosophy Fellowship, Inc., 1407 Chapala Street, Santa Barbara, California 93101. U.T.F. is a non-profit corporation established in 1969 with the following three charter objects: (1) to form the nucleus of a Universal Brotherhood of Humanity, without distinction of race, creed, sex, caste, color or condition; (2) the study of ancient and modern religions, philosophies and sciences, and the demonstration of the importance of such study; and (3) the investigation of the unexplained laws of Nature and the psychical powers latent in man.*

सत्यान्नास्ति परो धर्मः ।

THERE IS NO RELIGION HIGHER THAN TRUTH

KNOWLEDGE OF THE SELF 133

NUMBER AS DIVINE SCIENCE 138

PYTHAGOREAN HARMONICS IV:
GEOMETRY, NUMBER AND SOUND. . 139

MEASURE OF GRACE 151

REINCARNATION 152

THE SELF-IMPOSED TASK 167

IMAGINATION. 171

THE DIAMOND HEART 172

THE POINT 180

GLOSSARY 194

THE GAZE OF THE BUDDHA 196

KNOWLEDGE OF THE SELF

There is only one Perceiver; the sights are modified by the channels through which the Perceiver looks. It is the same Soul in any and all modifications. The power of seeing is the Soul; the power of the Soul goes into the seeing, hence what It "sees" is to It real because seen; as sights each is a reality; but the nature of Soul is different from any and all "sights."

The nature of Soul as unmodifiable must be grasped; then, each sight is perceived as a relativity and there is no more identification than we assume when we see the many thousands of things that are about us every day, unaffected, unless we concentrate upon them. We concentrate upon some things, automatically, through habitude; this automatic habit has to be gradually changed, and control substituted. It is to be effected by trying to do it, by keeping at it. The Mind as at present constituted is attracted or repelled by externalities, and the power of the Soul flows in the direction of concentration, be that long or short. Through the Mind, the Soul determines bad, good, better, best, on this or any plane. Mind has to be adjusted by knowledge of essential nature, of causes, and by analogies and correspondence. The views held in regard to existence constitute the Mind and direct the Soul's energy in that relation.

There is just "Consciousness" and its "states," which are conditioned consciousness. We speculate on conditions; we cannot on Consciousness itself, for we are that. We cannot find Ourselves in any kind or number of conditions, which are but pictures in the mind. "It is of this stairway that thou art the mirror and faithful climber" might mean climbing beyond conditions; is not that the "awakening of the Self" which the Upanishads speak of? A man in a dark room is conditioned by the darkness; in the open he is conditioned in other ways; but he is the same man. We must have knowledge in order to use power rightly, but we must know that we are neither knowledge nor power; they are ours; to imagine that we are any given knowledge or power is illusion. It might be said that there are two kinds of knowledge—knowledge of any and all conditions, and knowledge of the Self. Knowledge of the Self is beyond relativity; relativity cannot be known by relativity, but only by that which is beyond all relativity. "To blend thy Mind and Soul" is to make the Mind subservient to the purposes of Soul, an instrument for use, not a cage of relativities in which to imprison ourselves.

"No action from a true basis could proceed far in an erroneous direction" is right. Right basis is the compass; should wind or tide deflect the course, the compass is there to tell the story. We have many correct ideas in particulars, but forget the universal application of them. The fact that the Perceiver is One and Impartite, and that the "seeing" is looking directly on Ideas, is the basis of consideration. No idea is real, for on "looking" at it, motion is caused which spells "change." The change is not so much in the object of vision, as in the mode of seeing. We are so liable to imagine that the change is external, and endeavor to adjust externalities to internal change—an eternal and ineffectual struggle. We seek one of the pair of opposites, instead of finding the basis of their unity, because of our desires.

Kama-loka means the plane or place of Desire. Doubt and Desire seem to go together; for wanting a thing implies the doubt of getting it, and intensity of doubt is expressed in fear. So Desire, Doubt, and Fear are the characteristics of the *Kama-lokic* state. I think we may have these about anything in life, and in accordance with our intensity attract similar energies from the *Kama-lokic* state, whether emanating from living or dead personalities. Lengthy periods of doubt and fear are more intensive than shorter ones in their drawing power and subsequent effects. We enter that current and receive from that plane so long as we hold on to it. But there is the other side—we can desire nothing for ourselves and determine to accept what comes. Events and conditions come and go, and no amount of desiring will prevent their coming or hinder their going. Taking this attitude, we live in the Eternal and watch the wheel of Progress called change with neither desire, fear nor doubt to assail us.

When we desire anything, the thing itself is not what we want, but the feeling that the thing gives us; if the thing gave us no "feeling," we would not desire it. To do service is also "feeling," but how different in its effects—beneficial instead of harmful reactions.

What will we do when we hear and see what is in *Kama-loka*? I think that when we arrive at that stage, we shall know we are looking at a condition, and will not be identified with it, unless we should choose to plunge into it in order to "feel" the state. Those in it know nothing but the desires and passions which animate them, think of nothing else; to them there is no other state....

"To abstain from condemning others" is a course to be continually striven for; it is vital. No two really act from the same basis of perception; how then can anyone judge? It should be granted that each one is trying to do his best—the best that he knows. His knowledge may be small, but if he strives to do the best he knows, his knowledge increases. For myself, I have an end in view in what I do; not my end, but something which includes many others—all if possible. Whether a temple is intended or a building for a saloon, similar work has to be performed; so actions are no safe basis to judge from. As students get to understand this in regard to each other, each in his degree, better results may be confidently expected. We credit each other with the best of motives and let it go at that; any other way leads to confusion and misunderstanding, hence to separative thought and action.

"What do people get 'mad' about?" I think, generally, at something another has done, or failed to do; or at some fancied slight. We feel annoyed at the circumstances, really, not the person; although we foolishly confuse the two. Now a thing done, is done; no amount of irritation can change it. What is needed is a consideration of what led up to the doing; this should be taken up as calmly as any other proposition. If someone annoys you or irritates you by manner or action, it is to be assumed that he is not doing it on purpose to annoy. Try to understand his viewpoint; examine the man's machinery, just as you would a machine. Some people have been known to get mad at a machine, and feel destruction in regard to it; but where is the fault? The machine cannot learn anything; the man can, and needs to. The main trouble, I think, is that most people consider it perfectly proper to make their likes and dislikes a basis for action, everything being judged from that basis. This, of course, is altogether wrong, although very common. We are not called upon for judgment, but for right action; to act rightly ourselves, and by precept and example induce it in others. If we essay this task, it will at once appear that we cannot act rightly unless calmly. We have to cultivate Calmness under all circumstances. Calmness is like a rock; waves of irritation may dash at it, but cannot affect it; it can be attained by seeing the necessity for it, and by endeavor which is constant. It comes from "resting in the Real," which is never moved, but moves all things, sees all, without being involved.

So if we take all these things as just our "tryouts," we shall be able to get the right view of them, and the right attitude. These things in themselves do not matter; it does matter that we are unshaken. Of course, I am saying these things to myself, for you know them right well; only sometimes we forget and revert to habitude. But there is always that place which is never moved, to rest on and in. So with confidence in Them we go forward, and may Peace be ever ours.

"The Spirit in the Body" ROBERT CROSBIE
Letter Seventeen

NUMBER AS DIVINE SCIENCE

The Pythagorean understanding of Number is quite different from the predominantly quantitative understanding of today. For the Pythagoreans, Number is a living, qualitative reality which must be approached in an experiential manner. Whereas the typical modern usage of number is as a sign, to denote a specific quantity or amount, the Pythagorean usage is not, in a sense, even a usage at all: Number is not something to be used; rather its nature is to be discovered. In other words, we use numbers as tokens to represent things, but for the Pythagoreans Number is a universal principle, as real as light (electromagnetism) or sound...Because Pythagorean science possessed a sacred dimension, Number is seen not only as a universal principle, it is a divine principle as well. The two, in fact, are synonymous: because Number is universal it is divine; but one could as easily say that because it is divine, it is universal.

The Pythagorean Sourcebook and Library   DAVID FEDELER

PYTHAGOREAN HARMONICS IV

GEOMETRY, NUMBER AND SOUND

God geometrizes.

PLATO

From the very beginning of Æons — in time and space in our Round and Globe — the Mysteries of Nature... were recorded by the pupils of those same now invisible "heavenly men," in geometrical figures and symbols. The keys thereto passed from one generation of "wise men" to the other. Some of the symbols, thus passed from the east to the west, were brought therefrom by Pythagoras, who was not the inventor of his famous "Triangle." The latter figure, along with the plane, cube and circle, are more eloquent and scientific descriptions of the order of the evolution of the Universe, spiritual and psychic, as well as physical, than volumes of descriptive Cosmogonies and revealed *"Geneses."* The *ten points* inscribed within that "Pythagorean *triangle*" are worth all the theogonies and angelologies ever emanated from the theological brain. For he who interprets them — on their very face, and in the order given — will find in these seventeen points (the seven Mathematical Points hidden) the uninterrupted series of the genealogies from the first *Heavenly* to *terrestrial* man. And, as they give the order of Beings, so they reveal the order in which were evolved the Kosmos, our earth, and the primordial elements by which the latter was generated. Begotten in the invisible *Depths*, and in the womb of the same "Mother" as its fellow-globes — he who will master the mysteries of our Earth, will have mastered those of all others.

The Secret Doctrine i 612-613   H.P. BLAVATSKY

The importance of geometry to *Theosophia* cannot be overstated. H.P. Blavatsky called it "the Alpha and Omega of mystical conception" in its transcendental application to all seven of the divine sciences of the once universal Wisdom Religion. Like 'number', this Pythagorean approach to and understanding of geometry is vastly different than that of modern materialistic science. Quite apart from any utilitarian use or application in the study of visible nature, the most basic geometrical constructions such as the circle, triangle and square pertain to deific, immortal presences, both within and without. Like the sacred portraits given of the fully awakened Bodhisattva whose heart beats in unison with the logoic sound and light of the cosmos, they represent living moral and spiritual paradigms co-existent with the generative, unchanging and all-pervading foundations of life, their eternal beauty and wisdom surpassing all mutable objects made beautiful or comprehensible by them. So integral are they to spiritual awakening and self-transformation, wrote H.P.B., that the deeper levels of reality they pertain to are only obtained through initiation on the path of renunciation.

In typical chronologies of Western history, Euclid (c. 300 B.C.E.) is considered the "father of geometry" and one of the greatest mathematicians of antiquity. However, it is well known that he was a codifier and synthesizer, not an inventor or discoverer. And though it cannot be proven by extant documents, it is suggested by Sir Thomas Heath and Thomas Taylor that much if not all that is given in Euclid was passed down orally for centuries through the earliest Pythagoreans and formed a quintessential part of required study in the Platonic Academy. "Let no one ignorant of geometry enter here" was engraved over the door of Plato's school in Athens. Along with the Platonic dialogues, Theon of Smyrna (c. 120-140 C.E.), Nicomachus (c. 60-120 C.E.), and Iamblichus (c. 235-345 C.E.), Euclid provides us with one of the most important ancient sources of study regarding Pythagorean teaching.

It follows that in attempting to unfold some glimmer of the profound metaphysical and meta-psychological meanings associated with the famed Pythagorean decad of ten points, we could begin by constructing the graphic in a Euclidean manner while correlating the various stages with seed ideas drawn from *The Secret Doctrine*, the mythos of Greek antiquity and other traditions. This means beginning with a circle, upon which the entire super-structure of Pythagorean/Platonic cosmogony, of both meta-geometry and Euclidean geometry, is built. Ontologically prior to the drawn circle of bounded circumference, consciousness dwells in the unbounded sphere of abstract Space, the highest Deity passed over in silence by the Pythagoreans. Both void and plenum, it is the non-dual Reality called *Parabrahmam* or *Para-Vach* in Hindu philosophy, the *Shunyata* of Buddhism, "the face of the Deep" in Genesis, the Chaos (χάος) of Hesiod and Homer.

> The original Greek conception of Chaos is that of the Secret Wisdom Religion. In Hesiod, therefore, Chaos is infinite, boundless, endless and beginingless in duration, an abstraction at the same time as a visible presence...For in its etymological sense, Chaos is Space... (and) Space ... is the ever Unseen and Unknowable Deity in our philosophy.
>
> *Ibid*

To the finitizing mind this One Reality appears as darkness and absolute unconsciousness. To the awakened Seer it is a realm of absolute light. At the same time, this "center which is everywhere and circumference nowhere" should not be confused with the drawn circle. According to Nicomachus, the drawn circle is the Pythagorean *Monas*, meaning the Monad or One, associated with Apollo, whose name (*a-pollo*) means "without differentiation."

> The monad is the non-spatial source of all number ... holds seminally the principles which are within all numbers ... the beginning, middle and end of all things ... without which there is no knowledge of anything whatsoever, since it is a pure light, most authoritative over everything in general, and it is sun-like and ruling, so that in each of these respects it resembles God ... just as he made this universe harmonious and unified out of things which are likewise opposed.
>
> *The Theology of Arithmetic*   IAMBLICHUS

In the cosmogenesis of *The Secret Doctrine*, the Monad as primeval Unity is first linked with the unmanifested logos, the pre-cosmic origin of every kosmos initiated by the potential white point in the black circle. This Monad "which lives in solitude and darkness," is also without dimension, limits or boundaries. In the esoteric traditions within Northern Buddhism, H.P. Blavatsky correlates the unmanifested logos with *"Vajradhara"*, also known as *Dorje Chang* in Tibetan or *Adi-Buddha,* the Supreme Buddha. "As the Lord of all Mysteries he cannot manifest, but sends into the world of manifestation his heart—the 'diamond heart,' Vajrasattva." Similar to the myth of *Vishvakarman,* the entire kosmos is a singular essence which sacrificially manifests itself as the One Life in order to differentiate into the Great Chain of Being.

Simultaneous with the potential point is the diameter line of the circle called "Father-Mother", *Purusha-Prakriti, Prajna-Karuna,* from which proceeds the second logos, the manifested. Is this diameter line vertical or horizontal? If vertical, the 1 and the 0 is the number ten, pre-cosmic Ideation, the Heavenly Man. In Kabalistic terms, it is Adam Kadmon or the "Ancient of Days", both the origin and culmination of all human knowledge and the "androgyne synthesis of the creative builders" wholly latent in its omnipresent, pre-genetic glory. H.P. Blavatsky affirms that Pythagoras knew of the decimal system since the sacred spiritual science which he taught was built upon the number ten.

If the diameter line is horizontal, it is symbolic of pre-cosmic Substance, that of SVABHAVAT, "THE VOICE OF THE WORD" of Stanza IV. It is the unstruck Pythagorean monochord, divine mother nature, the Buddhist *Mulaprakriti,* the "Plastic Essence" which fills the universe, providing the material basis of every plane and form of embodiment. At this level of pre-cosmic unfoldment, matter and spirit, horizontal and vertical are identical in essence and expressed by the "X" or cross within the circle. Geometrically, both are needed in order to delineate an upright equilateral triangle within a given circle.

Fig. 1

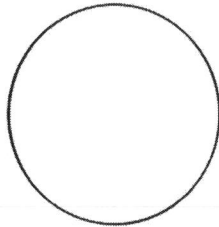

Fig. 2

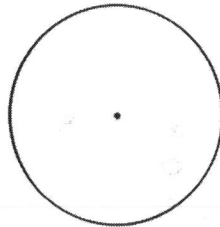

Fig. 3

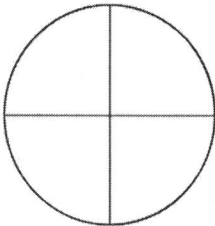

Fig. 4

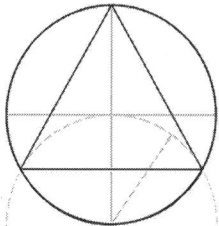

Fig. 5

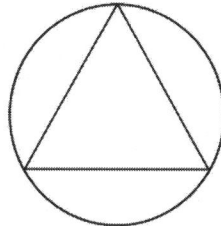

Fig. 6

"The first and Fundamental principle of Occultism is Universal Unity (or Homogeneity) under three aspects." "The Deity is one because it is infinite. It is triple because it is ever manifesting." In the Jewish mysticism of the Kabala, the first three formless emanations of the Sephirothal Tree, the Tree of Life and the source of noumenal nature are *Kether* (the Crown), *Binah* (Intelligence) and *Hokmah* (Wisdom). In Christianity, the theological trinity is Father, Son and Holy Spirit, while in the earliest known Vedas we find *Agni, Vayu* and *Surya.* This trinity became in the later Upanishads *Brahma, Vishnu,* and *Shiva,* and in Advaita Vedanta, *Sat-Chit-Ananda,* Truth-Consciousness-Bliss.

For the Pythagoreans, the triangle was the first true number and the first perfect space-enclosing geometrical figure associated with Proportion (*analogia*), Harmony, Knowledge, Piety and Friendship. In Greek antiquity, the third principle binding horizontal and vertical into a logoic triad is that of *Eros.* "As in the oldest Grecian Cosmogony, differing widely from the later mythology, Eros is the third person in the primeval trinity: Chaos, Gaea, Eros..." *Eros* is the highest aspect of Venus-Aphrodite, Divine Will, the Hindu *Kama-Deva* and the Tibetan *Fohat,* the active energy binding ideation to substance on every plane. As the highest expression of sacrificial compassion, it is "the propelling force, the active Power which causes the ONE to become TWO and THREE — on the Cosmic plane of manifestation." It is cosmic electricity guided by Universal Mind arising as primordial logoic light which heralds every dawn. All other noumenal or phenomenal forces are differentiations of that one Force which in Platonic thought causes the Universe itself to move with circular motion. In *The Secret Doctrine*, this *arupa* three-in-one (Spirit-Matter-Fohat), is the newly awakened Cosmic Mind, *Mahat,* or *Maha-Buddhi.*

> "...the Pythagorean Monad descending from "no-place" (*Aloka*), shoots like a falling star through the planes of non-being into the first world of being, and gives birth to Number One; then branching off, to the right, it produces Number Two; turning again to form the base-line it begets number Three, and thence ascending again to Number One, it finally disappears therefrom into the realms of non-being.
>
> *Ibid*

By mystic transmutation, wrote H.P.B., the three-in-one becomes a QUATERNARY, "the Triangle becomes "the TETRAKTYS" as "THE RADIANT ESSENCE BECOMES SEVEN INSIDE, SEVEN OUTSIDE." The Tetraktys is the combined luminous wisdom of countless suns, the oceanic immortal nectar harvested from an infinite series of previous cycles and holds *in potentia* all that will emerge in the current manvantara. This is connected with the deepest mysteries of *Manu* and *Manasaputra*. "Hence we learn in the "Commentaries" that while no Dhyan Chohan, not even the highest, can realize completely "the condition of the preceding Cosmic evolution," "the Manus retain a knowledge of their experiences of all the Cosmic evolutions throughout Eternity."

Conceptually and geometrically, there are a number of ways of visualizing this passage from three to four, triangle to tetrad. For example, the geometric fourth point may be understood as lying outside the triangle, equidistant from each of the three points already established and equal to the length of each side of the original triangle. In this way, the triangle becomes a tetrahedron, the simplest possible space enclosing three-dimensional form with six edges (Fig. 7). One equilateral triangle thereby transmutes into four. The tetrahedron is the only one of the five Platonic solids that is self-reciprocating. That is, if you take the center point of each face of the tetrahedron, an inner tetrahedron is formed, an inner seven, *ad infinitum*. In addition, the six edges of the tetrahedron correspond to the diagonals of each face of the six-sided cube or hexahedron, another geometrical symbol of the seven (Fig. 8). This process of unfoldment can be continued as the Kabalistic axiom states: the dodecahedron, "the whole of twelve faces," lies concealed within the perfect cube. When the cube is constructed within the dodecahedron, the sides of the cube are in golden ratio to the sides of the dodecahedron (Fig. 9).

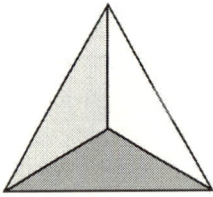

Fig. 7

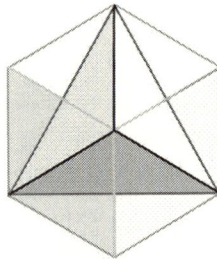

Fig. 8

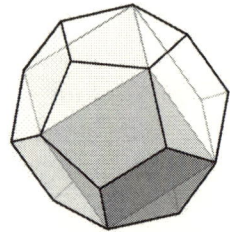

Fig. 9

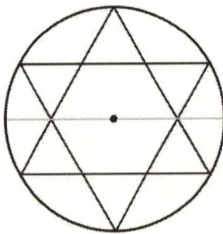

Fig. 10

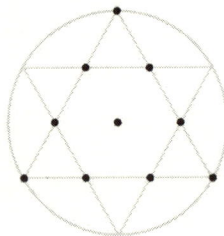

Fig. 11

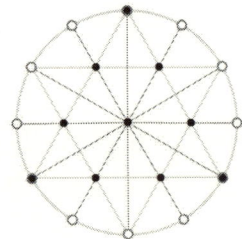

Fig. 12

Alternatively, the fourth point of the Tetraktys may be taken as the monadic center-point already established in the center of the two-dimensional triangle. Simultaneous with its diameter line, it provides a rotational laya center in which the upward pointing triangle is mirrored in a downward pointing triangle (Fig 10). In this way, 'above' is reflected 'below.' With the grid provided by the interlaced triangles and their common center point (the seventh), we can precisely locate the archetypal ten points of the Pythagorean decad (Fig 11). Furthermore, if we extend diameter lines from center to each nodal point thus defined, we arrive at a twelve-fold division of the perimeter circle pointing again to the "Twelve Great Orders" of the zodiac and *nidanas* (Fig 12).

All this begins to give us some understanding of why the Pythagoreans considered the Tetraktys to be both four, seven, and ten (the sum of the first four numbers). Having emerged in three steps from the one, it symbolized "the completion and perfection of Number," the elements of which all else is composed, called *Kosmos* (world-order), *Ouranos* (heaven) and *Pan* (the All). It was the all-inclusive archetype, which was believed to underlie every class of phenomena, bridging macrocosm and microcosm, as suggested by the eleven Tetrads that Theon of Smyrna listed. It represented self-conscious immortality and the highest wisdom, the sacrificial descent from One to Many and back again, the logoic heart and breath of nature by which the Pythagoreans swore their most sacred oaths. As Hierocles states in his commentary on *The Golden Verses,* "The Tetraktys contains and binds together all beginnings whatsoever, the elements, numbers, seasons, ages, societies and communities."

In relation to the teaching given in *The Voice of the Silence*, the four-fold Tetraktys could be fruitfully correlated with the two wings, head and tail of Kalahansa, the three-fold A-U-M of the *pranava* or *Gayatri* mantram. The logos itself and its light, *Daiviprakriti,* is linked in *The Secret Doctrine* with the *Madhyama* and *Pasyanti* forms of Vach. Rooted in *Nada Brahman,* the unstruck sound, the sacred Word is said to bind into one the seven eternities of Being (the white swan) and the seven of Non-Being (the

black swan). At the manvantaric dawn, this omnipresent
vibrational field periodically wakens and sustains every
spiritual atom, the entire monadic stream about to emerge
and differentiate through the seven Dhyanis into the seven
kingdoms of nature.

> "...geometrical figures...when closely studied,
> will yield not only a scientific explanation of the
> real, objective, existence of the "Seven sons of the
> divine Sophia," which is this light of the Logos,
> but show by means of other yet undiscovered
> keys that, with regard to Humanity, these "Seven
> Sons" and their numberless emanations, centres
> of energy personified, are an absolute necessity.
> Make away with them, and the mystery of Being
> and Mankind will never be unriddled, not even
> closely approached.
>
> *Ibid*

Through the monochord, Pythagoras also demonstrated
the correspondences of primary geometries with number
and sound. Although a single string represents a continuum
of tonal flux that may be infinitely divided, when plucked
certain harmonic nodal points innately occur. These nodal
points or consonances are determined by the ratios of the
first four whole numbers corresponding to 1/2, 1/3, 1/4, of
the total string. This series is the numeric or architectural
foundation of the diatonic musical scale of seven notes,
the basic "field" of which is the octave, 1:2, the doubling of
the vibrational frequency which inversely correlates with
the halving of the string. As one of the great luminaries
of the European Renaissance, Francesco Giorgio showed
in his treatise titled *Harmonia Mundi*, by utilizing the
octave of 6:12 one can arrive at whole number solutions
for the remainder of the scale. By further subdivision
through arithmetic and harmonic mediation one arrives at
the perfect fifth or 2:3 (6:9) and the perfect fourth or 3:4

(6:8), the two most powerful musical relationships. Thus, the consonances upon which the Greek musical system was based—octave, fifth and fourth—can be expressed by the progression 1:2:3:4, which also contains the composite consonances of the octave plus a fifth (1:2:3 or 6:12:18) and the two octaves (1:2:4 or 6:12:24). These were shown by Giorgio to correspond with the double and triple proportions given by Plato in the Timaeus as the fundamental divisions of order and harmony inherent in the cosmos and in the structure of the human soul.

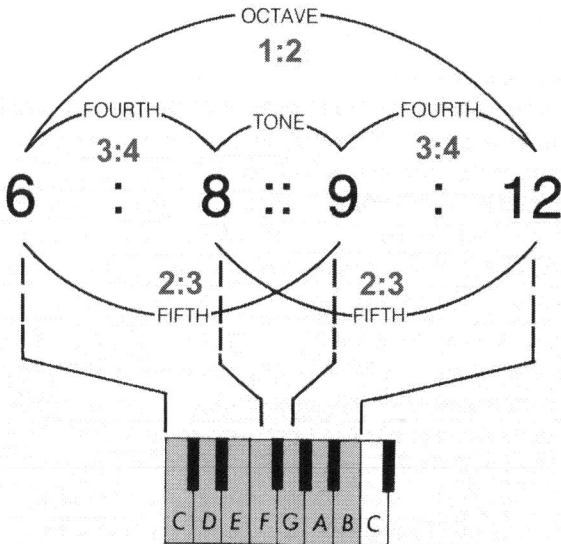

Nicomachus was a celebrated mathematician of the first century C.E., who wrote that astronomy, like music, is a science inspired by Pythagoras with mystical and theurgic properties, and that the motions of the stars and planets

1 Based on a similar illustration found in *The Pythagorean Sourcebook and Library*, Kenneth Sylvan Guthrie

150

have a perfectly melodious harmony. The harmonies of the seven sacred planets connected with the immortal gods could be reflected in earthly music and in human life, once the corresponding noetic principles had been awakened and activated. This inner, spiritual and ideational aspect of planetary motion is the famed music of the spheres retold in different ways by Cicero, by Plato and others. For more than 1600 years the idea was considered ridiculous and unscientific because of lack of supporting evidence. But modern science has begun to find that musical sounds are in fact emitted by heavenly bodies apparently due to differing oscillations in their atmospheres. They are inaudible to the human ear, but can be detected by scientific instruments. This is true not only of the earth, the sun and other planets, but also of galaxies. In 2003 a black hole in the Perseus galaxy cluster was found to be humming a drone 57 octaves below a middle C in the piano. According to NASA, this is roughly one million, billion times lower frequency than the human ear can detect.

> To the man who pursues his studies in the proper way, all geometric constructions, all systems of numbers, all duly constituted melodic progressions, the single ordered scheme of all celestial revolutions, should disclose themselves … by the revelation of a single bond of natural interconnection.
>
> *Plato*

To be continued.

MEASURE OF GRACE

And as to our own soul we are to hold that it stands, in part, always in the presence of the Divine, while in part it is concerned with the things of this sphere and in part occupies a middle ground. It is one nature in graded powers; and sometimes the soul in its entirety is borne along by the loftiest in itself; sometimes, the less noble part is dragged down and drags the mid-soul with it, though the law is that the soul may never succumb entire.

The soul's disaster falls upon it when it ceases to dwell in the perfect Beauty, thence to pour forth into the frame of the All whatsoever the All can hold of good and beauty. The measure of its absorption in that vision is the measure of its grace and power, and what it draws from this contemplation it communicates to the lower sphere, illuminated and illuminating always.

PLOTINUS

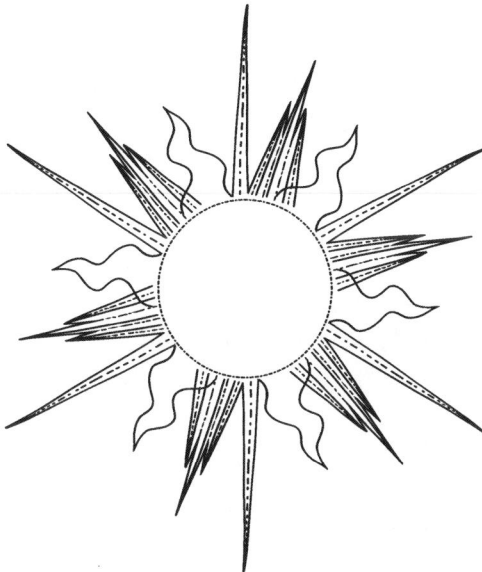

As the lord of this mortal frame experienceth
therein infancy, youth, and old age, so in future
incarnations will it meet the same. One who is
confirmed in this belief is not disturbed by anything
that may come to pass.

SRI KRISHNA

REINCARNATION

How man has come to be the complex being that he is and why, are questions that neither Science nor Religion makes conclusive answer to. This immortal thinker having such vast powers and possibilities, all his because of his intimate connection with every secret part of Nature from which he has been built up, stands at the top of an immense and silent evolution. He asks why Nature exists, what the drama of life has for its aim, how that aim may be attained. But Science and Religion both fail to give a reasonable reply. Science does not pretend to be able to give the solution, saying that the examination of things as they are is enough of a task; religion offers an explanation both illogical and unmeaning, and acceptable but to the bigot, as it requires us to consider the whole of Nature as a mystery and to seek for the meaning and purpose of life with all its sorrow in the pleasure of a God who cannot be found out. The educated and enquiring mind knows that dogmatic religion can only give an answer invented by man while it pretends to be from God.

What then is the universe for, and for what final purpose is man the immortal thinker here in evolution? It is all for the experience and emancipation of the soul, for the purpose of raising the entire mass of manifested matter up to the stature, nature, and dignity of conscious god-hood. The great aim is to reach self-consciousness; not through a race or a tribe or some favored nation, but by and through the perfecting, after transformation, of the whole mass of matter as well as what we now call soul. Nothing is or is to be left out. The aim for present man is his initiation into complete knowledge, and for the other kingdoms below him that they may be raised up gradually from stage to stage to be in time initiated also. This is evolution carried to its highest power; it is a magnificent prospect; it makes of man a god, and gives to every part of nature the possibility of being one day the same; there is strength and nobility in it, for by this no man is dwarfed and belittled, for no one is so originally sinful that he cannot rise above all sin. Treated from the materialistic position of Science, evolution takes in but half of life; while the religious conception of it is a mixture of nonsense and fear. Present religions keep the element of fear, and at the same time imagine that an Almighty being can think of no other earth but this and has to govern this one very imperfectly. But the old theosophical view makes the universe a vast, complete, and perfect whole.

Now the moment we postulate a double evolution, physical and spiritual, we have at the same time to admit that it can only be carried on by reincarnation. This is, in fact, demonstrated by science. It is shown that the matter of the earth and of all things physical upon it was at one time either gaseous or molten; that it cooled; that it altered; that from its alterations and evolutions at last were produced all the great variety of things and beings. This, on the physical plane, is transformation or change from one form to another. The total mass of matter is about the same as in the beginning of this globe, with a very minute allowance for some star dust. Hence it must have been changed over and over again, and thus been physically reformed and re-embodied. Of course, to be strictly accurate, we cannot use the word reincarnation, because "incarnate" refers to flesh. Let us say "re-embodied," and then we see that both for matter and for man there has been a constant change of form and this is, broadly speaking, "reincarnation." As to the whole mass of matter, the doctrine is that it will all be raised to man's estate when man has gone further on himself. There is no residuum left after man's final salvation which in a mysterious way is to be disposed of or done away with in some remote dust-heap of nature. The true doctrine allows for nothing like that, and at the same time is not afraid to give the true disposition of what would seem to be a residuum. It is all worked up into other states, for as the philosophy declares there is no inorganic matter whatever but that every atom is alive and has the germ of self-consciousness, it must follow that one day it will all have been changed. Thus what is now called human flesh is so much matter that one day was wholly mineral, later on vegetable, and now refined into human atoms. At a point of time very far from now the present vegetable matter will have been raised to the animal stage and what we now use as our organic or fleshy matter will have changed by transformation through evolution into self-conscious thinkers, and so on up the whole scale until the time shall come when what is now known as mineral matter will have passed on to the human stage and out into that of thinker. Then at the coming on of another great period of evolution the mineral matter of that time will be some which is now passing through its lower transformations on other planets and in other systems of worlds. This is perhaps a "fanciful" scheme for the men of the present day, who are so accustomed to being called bad, sinful, weak, and utterly foolish from their birth that they fear to believe the truth about themselves, but for the disciples of the ancient theosophists it is not impossible or fanciful, but is logical and vast. And no doubt it will one day be admitted by everyone when the mind of the western race has broken away from Mosaic chronology and Mosaic ideas of man and nature. Therefore as to reincarnation and metempsychosis we say that they are first to be applied to the whole cosmos and not alone to man. But as man is the most interesting object to himself, we will consider in detail its application to him.

This is the most ancient of doctrines and is believed in now by more human minds than the number of those who do not hold it. The millions in the East almost all accept it; it was taught by the Greeks; a large number of the Chinese now believe it as their forefathers did before them; the Jews thought it was true, and it has not disappeared from their religion; and Jesus, who is called the founder of Christianity, also believed and taught it. In the early Christian church it was known and taught, and the very best of the fathers of the church believed and promulgated it.

Christians should remember that Jesus was a Jew who thought his mission was to Jews, for he says in St. Matthew, "I am not sent but unto the lost sheep of the house of Israel." He must have well known the doctrines held by them. They all believed in reincarnation. For them Moses, Adam, Noah, Seth, and others had returned to earth, and at the time of Jesus it was currently believed that the old prophet Elias was yet to return. So we find, first, that Jesus never denied the doctrine, and on various occasions assented to it, as when he said that John the Baptist was actually the Elias of old whom the people were expecting. All this can be seen by consulting St. Matthew in chapters XVII, XI, and others.

In these it is very clear that Jesus is shown as approving the doctrine of reincarnation. And following Jesus we find St. Paul, in Romans IX, speaking of Esau and Jacob being actually in existence before they were born, and later such great Christian fathers as Origen, Synesius, and others believing and teaching the theory. In Proverbs VIII, 22, we have Solomon saying that when the earth was

156

made he was present, and that, long before he could have been born as Solomon, his delights were in the habitable parts of earth with the sons of men. St. John the Revelator says in Revs. III, 12, he was told in a vision which refers to the voice of God or the voice of one speaking for God, that whosoever should overcome would not be under the necessity of "going out" any more, that is, would not need to be reincarnated. For five hundred years after Jesus the doctrine was taught in the church until the Council of Constantinople. Then a condemnation was passed upon a phase of the question which has been regarded by many as against reincarnation, but if that condemnation goes against the words of Jesus it is of no effect. It does go against him, and thus the church is in the position of saying in effect that Jesus did not know enough to curse, as it did, a doctrine known and taught in his day and which was brought to his notice prominently and never condemned but in fact approved by him. Christianity is a Jewish religion, and this doctrine of reincarnation belongs to it historically by succession from the Jews, and also by reason of its having been taught by Jesus and the early fathers of the church. If there be any truthful or logical way for the Christian church to get out of this position—excluding, of course, dogmas of the church—the theosophist would like to be shown it. Indeed, the theosophist holds that whenever a professed Christian denies the theory he thereby sets up his judgment against that of Jesus, who must have known more about the matter than those who follow him. It is the anathema hurled by the church council and the absence of the doctrine from the teaching now that have damaged Christianity and made of all the Christian nations people who pretend to be followers of Jesus and the law of love, but who really as nations are followers of the Mosaic law of retaliation. For alone in reincarnation is the answer to all the problems of life, and in it and Karma is the force

that will make men pursue in fact the ethics they have in theory. It is the aim of the old philosophy to restore this doctrine to whatsoever religion has lost it; and hence we call it the "lost chord of Christianity."

But who or what is it that reincarnates? It is not the body, for that dies and disintegrates; and but few of us would like to be chained forever to such bodies as we now have, admitted to be infected with disease except in the case of the savage. It is not the astral body, for, as shown, that also has its term and must go to pieces after the physical has gone. Nor is it the passions and desires. They, to be sure, have a very long term, because they have the power to reproduce themselves in each life so long as we do not eradicate them. And reincarnation provides for that, since we are given by it many opportunities of slowly one by one, killing off the desires and passions which mar the heavenly picture of the spiritual man.

It has been shown how the passional part of us coalesces with the astral after death and makes a seeming being that has a short life to live while it is disintegrating. When the separation is complete between the body that has died, the astral body, and the passions and desires—life having begun to busy itself with other forms—the Higher Triad, *Manas, Buddhi,* and *Atma,* who are the real man, immediately go into another state, and when that state, which is called *Devachan,* or heaven, is over, they are attracted back to earth for reincarnation. They are the immortal part of us; they, in fact, and no other are we. This should be firmly grasped by the mind, for upon its clear understanding depends the comprehension of the entire doctrine. What stands in the way of the modern western man's seeing this clearly is the long training we have all had in materialistic science and materializing religion, both of which have made the mere physical body too prominent. The one has taught of matter alone and the other has preached the resurrection of the body, a doctrine against common sense, fact, logic, and testimony. But there is no doubt that the theory of the bodily resurrection has arisen from the corruption of the older and true teaching. Resurrection is founded on what Job says about seeing his redeemer in his flesh, and on St. Paul's remark that the body was raised incorruptible. But Job was an Egyptian who spoke of seeing his teacher or initiator, who was the redeemer, and Jesus and Paul referred to the spiritual body only.

Although reincarnation is the law of nature, the complete trinity of *Atma-Buddhi-Manas* does not yet fully incarnate in this race. They use and occupy the body by means of the entrance of *Manas,* the lowest of the three, and the other two shine upon it from above, constituting the God in Heaven. This was symbolized in the old Jewish teaching about the Heavenly Man who stands with his head in heaven and his feet in hell. That is, the head *Atma* and *Buddhi* are yet in heaven, and the feet, *Manas,* walk in hell, which is the body and physical life. For that reason man is not yet fully conscious, and reincarnations are needed to at last complete the incarnation of the whole trinity in the body. When that has been accomplished the race will have become as gods, and the godlike trinity being in full possession the entire mass of matter will be perfected and raised up for the next step. This is the real meaning of "the word made flesh." It was so grand a thing in the case of any single person, such as Jesus or Buddha, as to be looked upon as a divine incarnation. And out of this, too, comes the idea of the crucifixion, for *Manas* is thus crucified for the purpose of raising up the thief to paradise.

It is because the trinity is not yet incarnate in the race that life has so many mysteries, some of which are showing themselves from day to day in all the various experiments made on and in man.

The physician knows not what life is nor why the body moves as it does, because the spiritual portion is yet enshrouded in the clouds of heaven; the scientist is wandering in the dark, confounded and confused by all that hypnotism and other strange things bring before him, because the conscious man is out of sight on the very top of the divine mountain, thus compelling the learned to speak of the "subconscious mind," the "latent personality," and the like; and the priest can give us no light at all because he denies man's god-like nature, reduces all to the level of original sin, and puts upon our conception of God the black mark of inability to control or manage the creation without invention of expedients to cure supposed errors. But this old truth solves the riddle and paints God and Nature in harmonious colors.

Reincarnation does not mean that we go into animal forms after death, as is believed by some Eastern peoples. "Once a man always a man" is the saying in the Great Lodge. But it would not be too much punishment for some men were it possible to condemn them to rebirth in brute bodies; however, nature does not go by sentiment but by law, and we, not being able to see all, cannot say that the brutal man is brute all through his nature. And evolution having brought *Manas* the Thinker and Immortal Person on to this plane, cannot send him back to the brute which has not *Manas*.

By looking into two explanations for the literal acceptation by some people in the East of those laws of Manu which seem to teach the transmigrating into brutes, insects, and so on, we can see how the true student of this doctrine will not fall into the same error.

The first is that the various verses and books teaching such transmigration have to do with the actual method of reincarnation, that is, with the explanation of the actual physical processes which have to be undergone by the Ego in passing from the unembodied to the embodied state, and also with the roads, ways, or means of descent from the invisible to the visible plane. This has not yet been plainly explained in Theosophical books, because on the one hand it is a delicate matter, and on the other the details would not as yet be received even by Theosophists with credence, although one day they will be. And as these details are not of the greatest importance they are not now expounded. But as we know that no human body is formed without the union of the sexes, and that the germs of such production are locked up in the sexes and must come from food which is taken into the body, it is obvious that foods have something to do with the reincarnating of the Ego. Now if the road to reincarnation leads through certain foods and none other, it may be possible that if the Ego gets entangled in food which will not lead to the germ of physical reproduction, a punishment is indicated where Manu says that such and such practices will lead to transmigration, which is then a "hindrance." I throw this out so far for the benefit of certain theosophists who read these and whose own theories on this subject are now rather vague and in some instances based on quite other hypotheses.

The second explanation is, that inasmuch as nature intends us to use the matter which comes into our body and astral body for the purpose, among others, of benefiting the matter by the impress it gets from association with the human Ego, if we use it so as to give it only a brutal impression it must fly back to the animal kingdom to be absorbed there instead of being refined and kept on the human plane. And as all the matter which the human Ego gathered to it retains the stamp or photographic impression of the human being, the matter transmigrates to the lower level when given an animal impress by the Ego. This actual fact in the great chemical laboratory of nature could easily be misconstrued by the ignorant. But the present-day students know that once *Manas* the Thinker has arrived on the scene he does not return to baser forms; first, because he does not wish to, and second, because he cannot. For just as the blood in the body is prevented by valves from rushing back and engorging the heart, so in this greater system of universal circulation the door is shut behind the Thinker and prevents his retrocession. Reincarnation as a doctrine applying to the real man does not teach transmigration into kingdoms of nature below the human.

Unless we deny the immortality of man and the existence of soul, there are no sound arguments against the doctrine of pre-existence and re-birth save such as rest on the dictum of the church that each soul is a new creation. This dictum can be supported only by blind dogmatism, for given a soul we must sooner or later arrive at the theory of re-birth, because even if each soul is new on this earth it must keep on living somewhere after passing away, and in view of the known order of nature will have other bodies in other planets or spheres. Theosophy applies to the self—the thinker—the same laws which are seen everywhere in operation throughout nature, and those are all varieties of the great law that effects follow causes and no effect is without a cause. The soul's immortality—believed in by the mass of humanity—demands embodiment here or elsewhere, and to be embodied means reincarnation. If we come to this earth for but a few years and then go to some other, the soul must be embodied there as well as here, and if we have traveled from some other world we must have had there too our proper vesture. The powers of mind and the laws governing its motion, its attachment, and its detachment as given in theosophical philosophy show that its re-embodiment must be here, where it moved and worked, until such time as the mind is able to overcome the forces which chain it to this globe. To permit the involved entity to transfer itself to another scene of action before it had overcome all the causes drawing it here and without its having worked out its responsibilities to other entities in the same stream of evolution would be unjust and contrary to the powerful occult laws and forces which continually operate upon it. The early Christian Fathers saw this, and taught that the soul had fallen into matter and was obliged by the law of its nature to toil upward again to the place from which it came. They used an old Greek hymn which ran:

> **Eternal Mind, thy seedling spark,**
> **Through this thin vase of clay,**
> **Athwart the waves of chaos dark**
> **Emits a timorous ray.**
> **This mind enfolding soul is sown,**
> **Incarnate germ in earth:**

In pity, blessed Lord, then own
What claims in Thee its birth.
Far forth from Thee, thou central fire,
To earth's sad bondage cast,
Let not the trembling spark expire;
Absorb thine own at last!

Each human being has a definite character different from every other human being, and masses of beings aggregated into nations show as wholes that the national force and distinguishing peculiarities go to make up a definite and separate national character. These differences, both individual and national, are due to essential character and not to education. Even the doctrine of the survival of the fittest should show this, for the fitness cannot come from nothing but must at last show itself from the coming to the surface of the actual inner character. And as both individuals and nations among those who are ahead in the struggle with nature exhibit an immense force in their character, we must find a place and time where the force was evolved. These, Theosophy says, are this earth and the whole period during which the human race has been on the planet.

So, then, while heredity has something to do with the difference in character as to force and morale, swaying the soul and mind a little and furnishing also the appropriate place for receiving reward and punishment, it is not the cause for the essential nature shown by every one.

But all these differences, such as those shown by babes from birth, by adults as character comes forth more and more, and by nations in their history, are due to long experience gained during many lives on earth, are the outcome of the soul's own evolution. A survey of one short human life gives no ground for the production of his inner nature. It is needful that each soul should have all possible experience, and one life cannot give this even under the best conditions. It would be folly for the Almighty to put us here for such a short time, only to remove us just when we had begun to see the object of life and the possibilities in it. The mere selfish desire of a person to escape the trials and discipline of life is not enough to set nature's laws aside, so the soul must be reborn until it has ceased to set in motion the cause of rebirth, after having developed character up to its possible limit as indicated by all the varieties of human nature, when every experience has been passed through, and not until all of truth that can be known has been acquired. The vast disparity among men in respect to capacity compels us, if we wish to ascribe justice to Nature or to God, to admit reincarnation and to trace the origin of the disparity back to the past lives of the Ego. For people are as much hindered and handicapped, abused and made the victims of seeming injustice because of limited capacity, as they are by reason of circumstances of birth or education. We see the uneducated rising above circumstances of family and training, and often those born in good families have very small capacity; but the troubles of nations and families arise from want of capacity more than from any other cause. And if we consider savage races only, there the seeming injustice is enormous. For many savages have good actual brain capacity, but still are savage. This is because the Ego in that body is still savage and undeveloped, for in contrast to the savage there are many civilized men with small actual brain force who are not savage in nature because the indwelling Ego has had long experience in civilization during other lives, and being a more developed soul has power to use the brain instrument to its highest limit.

Each man feels and knows that he has an individuality of his own, a personal identity which bridges over not only the gaps made by sleep but also those sometimes supervening on temporary lesions in the brain. This identity never breaks from beginning to end of life in the normal person, and only the persistence and eternal character of the soul will account for it.

So, ever since we began to remember, we know that our personal identity has not failed us, no matter how bad may be our memory. This disposes of the argument that identity depends on recollection, for the reason that if it did depend alone on recollection we should each day have to begin over again, as we cannot remember the events of the past in detail, and some minds remember but little yet feel their personal identity. And as it is often seen that some who remember the least insist as strongly as the others on their personal identity, that persistence of feeling must come from the old and immortal soul.

Viewing life and its probable object, with all the varied experience possible for man, one must be forced to the conclusion that a single life is not enough for carrying out all that is intended by Nature to say nothing of what man himself desires to do. The scale of variety in experience is enormous. There is a vast range of powers latent in man which we see may be developed if opportunity be given. Knowledge infinite in scope and diversity lies before us, and especially in these days when special investigation is the rule. We perceive that we have high aspirations with no time to reach up to their measure, while the great troop of passions and desires, selfish motives and ambitions, war with us and among themselves, pursuing us even to the door of death. All these have to be tried, conquered, used, subdued. One life is not enough for all this. To say that we have but one life here with such possibilities put before us and impossible of development is to make the universe and life a huge and cruel joke perpetrated by a powerful God who is thus accused, by those who believe in a special creation of souls, of triumphing and playing with puny man just because that man is small and the creature of the Almighty. A human life at most is seventy years; statistics reduce this to about forty; and out of that little remainder a large part is spent in sleep and another part in childhood. Thus in one life it is perfectly impossible to attain to the merest fraction of what Nature evidently has in view. We see many truths vaguely which a life gives us no time to grasp, and especially is this so when men have to make such a struggle to live at all. Our faculties are small or dwarfed or weak; one life gives no opportunity to alter this; we perceive other powers latent in us that cannot possibly be brought out in such a small space of time; and we have much more than a suspicion that the extent of the field of truth is vastly greater than the narrow circle we are confined to. It is not reasonable to suppose that either God or nature projects us into a body simply to fill us with bitterness because we can have no other opportunity here, but rather we must conclude that a series of incarnations has led to the present condition, and that the process of coming here again and again must go on for the purpose of affording us the opportunity needed.

The Ocean of Theosophy, 60–69, 79–83   W. Q. JUDGE

Power surrounds necessity.
PYTHAGORAS

The great and peaceful ones live regenerating the
world like the coming of the spring; having crossed
the ocean of embodied existence themselves, they
freely aid all others who seek to cross it. The very
essence and inherent will of Mahatmas is to remove
the suffering of others, just as the ambrosia-rayed
moon of itself cools the earth heated by the intense
rays of the sun.

SHANKARACHARYA

THE SELF-IMPOSED TASK

The Occult Science is *not* one, in which secrets can be communicated of a sudden, by a written or even verbal communication. If so, all the 'Brothers' should have to do, would be to publish a *Hand-book* of the art which might be taught in schools as grammar is. It is the common mistake of people that we willingly wrap ourselves and our powers in mystery—that we wish to keep our knowledge to ourselves, and of our own will refuse—"wantonly and deliberately" to communicate it. The truth is that till the neophyte attains to the condition necessary for that degree of Illumination to which, and for which he is entitled and fitted, most *if not all* of the Secrets are *incommunicable*. The receptivity must be equal to the desire to instruct. The illumination must come from within. Till then no hocus pocus of incantations, or mummery of appliances, no metaphysical lectures or discussions, no self-imposed penance can give it. All these are but means to an end, and all we have to do is to direct the use of such means as have been empirically found by the experience of ages to conduce to the required object.

And this was and has been no secret for thousands of years. Fasting, meditation, chastity of thought, word, and deed; silence for certain periods of time to enable nature herself to speak to him who comes to her for information: government of the animal passions and impulses; utter unselfishness of intention, the use of certain incense and fumigations for physiological purposes, have been published as the means since the days of Plato and Iamblichus in the West, and since the far earlier times of our Indian Rishis. How these must be complied with to suit each individual temperament is of course a matter for his own experiment and the watchful care of his tutor or Guru. Such is in fact part of his course of discipline, and his Guru or initiator can but assist him with his experience and will power but can do no more until the last and Supreme initiation.

I am also of opinion that few candidates imagine the degree of inconvenience—nay suffering and harm to himself—the said initiator submits to for the sake of his pupil. The peculiar physical, moral, and intellectual conditions of neophytes and Adepts alike vary much, as anyone will easily understand; thus, in each case, the instructor has to adapt his conditions to those of the pupil, and the strain is terrible for to achieve success we have to bring ourselves into a full rapport with the subject under training. And as, the greater the powers of the Adept the less he is in sympathy with the natures of the profane who often come to him saturated with the emanations of the outside world, those animal emanations of the selfish, brutal, crowd that we so dread the longer he was separated from that world and the purer he has himself become, the more difficult the self-imposed task. Then knowledge, can only be communicated gradually; and some of the highest secrets if actually formulated even in your well prepared ear might sound to you as insane gibberish, notwithstanding all the sincerity of your present assurance that "absolute trust defies misunderstanding." This is the real cause of our reticence. This is why people so often complain with a plausible show of reason that no new knowledge is communicated to them, though they have toiled for it for two, three or more years. Let those who really desire to learn abandon all and come to us, instead of asking or expecting us to go to them. But how is this to be done in your world, and atmosphere? "Woke up sad on the morning of the 18th." Did you? Well, well, patience, my good brother, patience. Something bas occurred, though you have preserved no consciousness of the event; but let this rest. Only what more can I do? How am I to give expression to ideas for which you have as yet no language? The finer and more susceptible heads get like yourself, more than others do, and even when they get a little extra dose it is lost for want of words and images to fix the floating ideas, Perhaps, and undoubtedly you know not to what I now refer to. You will know it one day—Patience. To give more knowledge to a man than he is yet fitted to receive is a dangerous experiment; and furthermore, other considerations go to restrain me. The sudden communication of facts, so transcending the ordinary, is in many instances fatal not only to the neophyte but to those directly about him. It is like delivering an infernal machine or a cocked and loaded revolver into the hands of one who had never seen such a thing. Our case is exactly analogous. We feel that the time is approaching, and that we are bound to choose between the triumph of Truth or the Reign of Error-and-Terror. We have to let in a few chosen ones into the great secret.... Having then, to deliver with one hand the much needed yet dangerous weapon to the world, and with the other to keep off the Shammars (the havoc produced by them already being immense) do you not think we have a right to hesitate, to pause and feel the necessity of caution, as we never did before? To sum up: the misuse of knowledge by the pupil always reacts upon the initiator; nor, do I believe you know yet, that in sharing his secrets with another, the Adept by immutable Law, is delaying his own progress to the Eternal Rest. Perhaps, what I now tell you, may help you to a truer conception of things, and to appreciate our mutual position the better. Loitering on the way, does not conduce to a speedy arrival at the journey's end. And, it must strike you as a truism, that a Price must be paid for everything and every truth by somebody and in this case WE pay it.

MAHATMA K. H.

Seek for wisdom with obeisance, by questioning, and through service; the wise who see the Truth will instruct thee in the way of wisdom.

Knowing which, thou shalt not again fall into delusion, O son of Pandu; and in this way, thou shalt see all beings unreservedly in the Self, and thus in Me.

Bhagavad Gita IV, 34 - 35

IMAGINATION

This spiritual Love acts not
    nor can exist
Without Imagination,
    which, in truth,
Is but another name for
    absolute power
And clearest insight,
    amplitude of mind,
And Reason in her most
    exalted mood.
This faculty hath been the
    feeding source
Of our long labour: we have
    traced the stream
From the blind cavern
    whence is faintly heard
Its natal murmur; followed it to light
And open day; accompanied its course
Among the ways of Nature, for a time
Lost sight of it bewildered and engulfed;
Then given it greeting as it rose once more
In strength, reflecting from its placid breast
The works of man and face of human life;
And lastly, from its progress have we drawn
Faith in life endless, the sustaining thought
Of human Being, Eternity, and God.

WILLIAM WORDSWORTH

THE DIAMOND HEART

> *In the esoteric, and even exoteric Buddhism of the North,* Adi Buddha...*the One unknown, without beginning or end, identical with* Parabrahm *and* Ain-Soph, *emits a bright ray from its darkness. This is the Logos (the first), or* Vajradhara, *the Supreme Buddha (also called* Dorjechang). *As the Lord of all Mysteries he cannot manifest, but sends into the world of manifestation his heart — the "diamond heart,"* Vajrasattva (Dorjesempa).
> *The Secret Doctrine* i 571

In the Yogacharya tradition of Mahayana Buddhism, *Maha-Karuna,* meaning the 'Great Compassion', is the highest aspect of that non-dual Reality which transcends and pervades both Nirvana and Samsara. In the Lankavatara Sutra, this 'Pure Love' is defined as the culmination of the highest form of enlightenment expressing itself in the fully realized Buddha nature as *Prajna Paramita,* omniscient divine wisdom. This fusion of the highest compassion and wisdom, symbolized in Tibetan Buddhism as the union of vajra and bell, leads to the most exalted ideal known to us, the Diamond-Hearted Master of Wisdom, called *Vajrasattva;* indestructible, self-conscious immortality shining forth with skillful means into life after life for the benefit of sentient beings on behalf of universal enlightenment and felicity.

The Sanskrit word for kindness is *maitri* or in Pali: *metta.* It literally means 'friendship', but is often translated as 'loving-kindness'. *Maitri* is the cultivation of an active interest in the happiness of all other beings, whether they are perceived as enemies, friends or neither, and whether suffering appears to be present or not. In all schools of Buddhism, it is the first of what is called the "Four

Immeasurables" based on a meditative practice prescribed by the Buddha.

> He lets his mind pervade one quarter of the world with thoughts of loving kindness, and so the second, and so the third, and so the fourth. And thus the whole wide world, above, below, around, everywhere and equally, he continues to pervade with a heart of loving kindness, abundant, grown great, and without measure, without any taint of hostility or ill-will.
>
> *Samyuta Nikaya*

The other three Immeasurables are: Compassion *(Karuna),* Joy *(Mudita)* and Equanimity *(Upeksha).* Briefly described, *Mudita* or Joy is an impartial, inward rejoicing in the success and good fortune of others, a buoyant ever-flowing stream of unmitigated jubilance in the happiness and virtues realized by others as in all beneficial forms of karmic flourishing. *Upeksha* in this context is equanimity, a state of inner equipoise that is indifferent to personal gain or loss, honor or dishonor, praise or blame, pleasure or pain. It is meant to lead to freedom from all forms of egoistic self-reference and impatience. It is the capacity "to look upon tempests" and not be shaken, to witness with the eye of soul the vast suffering of humanity without fear, despair, depression, the wish for retaliation, or loss of confidence.

Each of the Immeasurables is to be consciously cultivated towards all beings in each of the six directions of space, until all space is pervaded and suffused with the elixir of pure benevolence and indestructible good will. This practice is not only one of the antidotes to selfishness and self-interest but also one which becomes in time, a fohatic instrument for dispelling all adverse influences. The Diamond Hearted is the holder of the *dorje* or *vajra.*

> *Dorje* is the Sanskrit *Vajra,* a weapon or instrument in the hands of some gods...and is

> regarded as having the same Occult power of
> repelling evil influences by purifying the air as
> Ozone in chemistry. It is also a Mudra, a gesture
> and posture used in sitting for meditation. It is
> in short, a symbol of power over invisible evil
> influences, whether as a posture or talisman...
> With the "Yellow Caps," or Gelugpas, it is
> a symbol of power, as the Cross is with the
> Christians.
>
> *The Voice of the Silence,* p. 59

The four-fold vajra progressively transforms consciousness and imagination into a sublime and highly potent
creative force. This is why the Four Immeasurables are
also called *Brahmā Viharas,* the "sublime or divine abodes
of *Brahmā.*" Brahmā as one aspect of the Hindu Trimurti,
is the highest creative deity, logos or Platonic *Demiurgos.*
In *The Voice of the Silence* this force culminates in an
abolute compassion that transcends lifetimes, eternities,
and manvantaras, participating in every logoic unfoldment.

> Behold! Thou has become the Light, thou has
> become the Sound, thou art thy Master and thy
> God. Thou art THYSELF the object of thy search:
> the VOICE unbroken, that resounds throughout
> eternities, exempt from change, from sin exempt,
> the Seven Sounds in one, THE VOICE OF THE
> SILENCE.
>
> *Ibid,* pp. 23-24

Although many concepts found within Mahayana
and Vajrayana Buddhism can be found in *The Voice of the
Silence,* according to H.P. Blavatsky, this small series
of fragments represents a universal "Trans-Himalayan"
esoteric tradition not confined to Buddhism. At the same
time, it may have been in the hidden libraries and retreat
of the Eighth Panchen Lama in the vicinity of Tashi Lunpo
that H.P.B, in the company of Masters, was given access to
the texts central to the translation of *The Voice of the Silence*

and the Stanzas of *Dzyan* as found in *The Secret Doctrine.* For the first time in known Western history, these truly esoteric texts were translated and partially made public by her. The Centenary edition of *The Voice of the Silence,* published in 1989, contains a dedication in Tibetan by the Ninth Panchen Lama and a forward by the 14th Dalai Lama. This certainly underlines the faithful reflection of aspects of esoteric *Theosophia* in Northern Buddhism. Moreover, exoterically it was in the Mahayana traditions of Buddhism that the cultivation of altruism, creative imagination, and logoic compassion were brought to center stage and focus in the eighth century *Bodhicharyavatara, The Guide to the Bodhisattva Way of Life* by Shantideva.

According to traditional biographical accounts, Shantideva was regarded by his fellow monks at Nalanda as a ne'er-do-well, whose behavior seemed restricted to activities of eating, sleeping and puttering around. In an effort to embarrass him, the monks invited a large congregation of people to the monastery and had the Abbot demand that he preach to them. Much to the monk's surprise, Shantideva responded by saying, "Would you like me to expound the teaching of a former scholar...or would you prefer me to recite something you have never heard?" The monks, chuckling to themselves and hoping to compound his embarrassment, replied, "Please teach us something completely new!" In response, Shantideva sounded the *Bodhicharyavatara,* which is said to be the entire teaching of the Buddha from the *Madhyamika* (Middle Way) perspective, all three turnings of the wheel delivered in a single, highly condensed poetic discourse. Moreover, during the exposition, it is said that the celestial Bodhisattva of wisdom, Manjushri, appeared seated in the sky. As the poem neared its end, both Shantideva and Manjushri ascended and disappeared into the clouds, Shantideva's voice alone resounding to the last verse.

The poetic sutra he recited became one of the great classics of Mahayana literature and according to Tibetan scholars, it the most widely read, cited, and practiced sutra in the whole of the Indo-Tibetan tradition. In 1984, when the Dalai Lama was presented with an English translation of the text and asked to bless it, he did so readily, placing it on his forehead saying, "If I have any understanding of compassion and the practice of the bodhisattva path, it is entirely on the basis of this text that I possess it."

The foundation of the path as given by Shantideva, is the cultivation of *bodhichitta,* a word rich in profound meaning, but which we may provisionally define as "the altruistic mind of enlightenment," the relinquishment of the very idea of individual salvation or spiritual freedom, replaced by the motivation to rescue all sentient beings from the darkness of ignorance and suffering. In this way, the seed of *bodhichitta* is linked with the highest form of loving-kindness, condensing the four Immeasurables into a single heart essence.

Over the centuries, many renowned Buddhist teachers have composed commentaries, frequently dividing Shantideva's text into three main sections, along the lines of a famous prayer attributed to Nagarjuna.

> **May *Bodhichitta*, precious and sublime,**
> **Arise where it has not yet come to be;**
> **And where it has arisen may it never fail**
> **But grow and flourish ever more and more.**

Following this scheme, the first three chapters are designed to stimulate the dawning of *bodhichitta* in the mind. The following three give instruction on how to prevent it from dissipating, while the seventh, eighth, and ninth propose the means by which *bodhichitta* may be progressively intensified. Chapter three contains the

Bodhisattva Vow, an extended version of the Kwan Yin Pledge which has since the eighth century been the words by which both laypersons and Tibetan Buddhist monks officially enter upon the Bodhisattva path. A portion of that vow is given below. The six chapters that follow give a detailed exposition on the *paramitas,* reinforcing the nature of the path also found in *The Voice of the Silence.* That is, that the highest form of enlightenment is realized through the cultivation of these 'transcendent excellences' by which consciousness is not only alchemized, transformed and elevated to the "other shore" of Nirvana, but by which the Heart Doctrine is embodied, thereby bridging heaven and earth, eternity and time. This involves the gestation of what Theosophy refers to as the permanent astral, or the *Nirmanakaya* robe which, like all esoteric human principles is in actuality, seven-fold. It is by this sublime means that the boundless mercy of Kwan Yin never ceases hearing the cries of humanity and by which it is capable of endlessly aiding the evolution of sentient beings "for *Kalpas* without number."

In following this path, one aspires to become like a stone in the Guardian Wall, serving the Boundless Light or Boundless Age of *Amitabha,* the great Brotherhood of Buddhas and Bodhisattvas who protect, sustain and guide all beings to their highest good. It is in this way that 'relative' or 'aspirational' *bodhichitta* is transformed into 'ultimate' *Bodhichitta* or Absolute Compassion where self and other, nirvana and samsara, unite and where the personal will is replaced by "the pure bright essence of *Alaya*", the universal will of SPACE itself, which knows no term, cessation, or decay.

> **And so I join my hands and pray**
> **The Buddhas who reside in every quarter:**
> **Kindle now the Dharma's light**
> **For those who grope, bewildered, in the dark of**
>   **suffering!**

For all those ailing in the world,
Until their every sickness has been healed,
May I myself become for them
The doctor, nurse, the medicine itself.

Raining down a flood of food and drink,
May I dispel the ills of thirst and famine.
And in the ages marked by scarcity and want,
May I myself appear as drink and sustenance.

For sentient beings, poor and destitute,
May I become a treasure ever plentiful,
And lie before them closely in their reach,
A varied source of all that they might need.

May I be a guard for those who need protection,
A guide for those who journey on the road.
For those who wish to go across the water,
May I be a boat, a raft, a bridge.

May I be the wishing jewel, the vase of plenty,
A word of power and the supreme healing;
May I be the tree of miracles,
And for every being the abundant cow.

Like the earth and the all-pervading elements,
Enduring as space itself endures,
For boundless multitudes of living beings,
May I be their ground and sustenance.

                                   SHANTIDEVA

THE POINT

•

Parallel projection can be regarded as a special case of central projection in which the centre of projection is an infinitely distant point.

DAVID HILBERT and STEPHAN COHN-VOSSEN

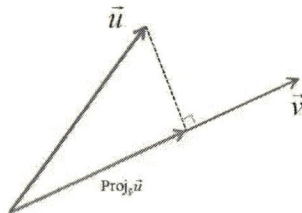

I
n asking about the point of this, one is tempted to expand the question in order to ponder the point of anything at all. A pointless pursuit, you say? Well yes, and yet one might point out that there is a point reached in every thinker's career when one confronts the question of basic meaning point-blank, as it were. This, of course, does not necessarily engender a sharpening of the wit or that gift for making the pointed remark so assiduously cultivated by the smart set. Nor does it tend to enhance one's ability to score points in the endlessly absorbing contest of social gamesmanship. As a matter of fact, persons having reached the point of bewilderment appear abstracted, confused and lost, as though they could use a compass to point their way out of the puzzlement. A new tack, a fresh point of view perhaps? Not their strong point, you say? One can advise forgetting the whole problem, but it may be pointed out that

at the point of death the point in question will inevitably assert itself and one might just as well tackle it, sit down on the old needle-point, and focus the mind on an infinitely distant and invisible point. What's the point of that, you say? Ah yes ... it does seem that we have come full circle back to the starting-point.

Origin, unity, the centre.... That is what the point symbolizes. It represents the principles of emanation and manifestation and it is that around which everything revolves. Alone and unmoved, it contains the totality of all possibilities and the human mind constantly intuits its primacy. Every phrase admonishing one to stick to the point, get back to the main point, or make a point of doing something contains within it an underlying awareness of a seminal core to things which is unvarying and original. Somehow the simplest mind apprehends that all lines which terminate in the circumference of a circle begin from a central point, and that any set of circumstances can be traced back to some such cause. This is true even at the most relative level and is consciously experienced by whole societies of human beings who perceive reality in relation to certain meaningful principles which rest at the very heart of their collective enterprise. Ortega y Gasset expressed this neatly when he wrote that "the choice of a point of view is the initial act of a culture".

The point at the centre of all things is sacred because it remains unmoved and because it is an axis which links the unmanifest with the manifest. In one way or another, thinkers from all cultures have conceived of that archetypal point as the Pivot of the Law, the basis of interaction between the three worlds. The outbreathing and inbreathing of the universe and all the centrifugal and centripetal action in phenomenal nature can be traced back ultimately to it. Everything emerges from it, revolves around it and returns to it, and it or one of its myriad progeny will be the reference point that lends order and meaning to all patterns of change in the world. It is because of this axis, this zero point, that man possesses any sense of time or space. Without a glimmering awareness of a still point within him and within the universe surrounding him, man would not experience a conscious sense of direction or of sequence. Like an animal, he would feel and act in accordance with the Law as it expresses itself through his nature: unquestioned, unexamined, unfettered by any conscious design. Instead, man orients his beliefs and his sense of order to some sort of pole-star. He departs in action from a point of beginning and returns to that point repeatedly in his efforts to understand the direction of his movement. The human mind thus charts its course, and an inevitable expression of this continual tendency can be found in the invention of the pivotal compass, whose magnetic needle is freely suspended at its central point of gravity. This instrument acts as a linking mechanism between man and the vast physical world around him, for, though he can use his movable sight to establish his own relative bearing, the needle will align itself to the total magnetic field vector and establish his position relative to the polar point.

There are two kinds of points; that which has no magnitude at all, which is metaphysical, and that which has the smallest conceivable magnitude and is manifest. The latter is a point in time and space, whilst the unmanifest answers to what the Hindus call 'the point beyond time', or Pure Being, in the language of the Taoists. Though incomprehensible to the finite mind, it is the point of equilibrium and harmony at the centre of the phenomenal universe. The Hebrews called it Shekinah, the central presence of God, and in the Islamic tradition it is revered as the Divine Abode, the eye of the Heart. The idea of this point provides the basis upon which is formulated all notions we have regarding degree. In the words of Moses de Leon, "This degree is the sum total of all subsequent mirrors, that is, of all external aspects related to this one degree. They proceed therefrom because of the mystery of the point, which is itself an occult degree emanating from the mystery of the pure and awe-inspiring ether. The first degree of all is absolutely occult, that is, not manifest, and cannot be attained."

The problem of understanding the relation between the One Point and the many has fascinated philosophers for millennia. This becomes particularly absorbing when the point is viewed as a symbol of unity and, therefore, the Good. Proclus observed that "The more complete is the cause of more, in proportion to the degree of its completeness: for the more complete participates in the Good more fully ... it is nearer to the Good ... the cause of all." This implies that the closer one moves towards the metaphysical, central point of existence, the greater the ability to act as a channel for the Good. But where is that centre and how does an individual recognize it in time and space?

Peasants all over the world intuitively recognize its presence in the seed they plant in the earth. The Hopi tenderly handle the maize seed in their hands and speak to the spirit within it whilst placing it in the soil. They recognize a point of immortality within the seed, a germ which never dies through all the cycles of sowing and reaping. They handle thousands of seeds and yet they salute this one same germinal spirit in each. Perhaps they intuit the relation between the One Point and the many. Artists also may sense something concerning this in their perception of the light inherent in each daub of paint. Neo-Impressionists and Pointillists developed this idea to a high degree. Painters like Georges Seurat displayed an unerring sense of relationship between tones, intervals and accents on the basis of individual points containing varying degrees of white mixed with colour. Seurat was fascinated with the study of space, perspective, light and the sensation of air moving around objects. Each point in his complex canvases contains within it the capability of expressing these elements, but it is only together as a whole pattern that they are able to manifest them clearly. It is when viewing the mass of points from a proper distance that one can grasp the more general point of the painting as envisioned by its creator.

Inspired by the ideas of the Pythagoreans and neo-Platonists, Renaissance thinkers paid homage in poetry and prose to the symbolism of the point. They echoed the ancient observance regarding the circle, which was said to have its circumference nowhere and its central point everywhere. Some, like Pelletier, recognized that "Unity, which represents the Point in geometry, is not Number, but only the origin of number." These two ideas allude to the mystery that shrouds the One Point which stands at the threshold dividing the noumenal and phenomenal planes. On a more commonplace level, a typical definition of the point goes back to Euclid, who declared that it was that which had no parts. This sort of mathematical definition asserts nothing about the existence or non-existence of the thing defined. It only suggests that it is possible to have an intuition of what a thing is and that its existence can be proved when it is shown why it exists by means of a construction. The essence of the point was never questioned by Euclid nor by Aristotle. They did not consider the point to be a reflection of an ideal or an eternal paradigm, nor did they attempt to take their analysis beyond assertion or proof to discover how the ultimate principles of the One and the Dyad account for points and lines and other figures.

> To see a solid body in a point must have its
> ground in a point, which has no point, if one
> thinks it over.
>
> EDOUARD DU MONIN

With certain refinements in thinking linked to a less
mechanical view of nature, more recent mathematicians
tend to view the point as the *minima visibilia,* supposing
an infinitely fine vision. One imagines an infinite division
of the atom, perhaps, and that congruence is the intuitive
connection of their couples. The singular point is the
one expression that is always present in all systems of
geometry. "While primitive relations vary, the fundamental
terms, namely points, remain always the same." Points
would seem thus to be the one indispensable element of
geometry, and yet one may ask if they are closer to nature
than volumes. Is our perception of points only possible
when they are big enough to be seen, or must we predicate
a paradigmatic realm where the question of volume does
not arise? When does the geometry of points become that
of volumes, or are they translatable? In an ideal realm, is
substance homogeneity or is there a subtle heterogeneity
involving points and breadth and depth?

In the phenomenal and highly heterogeneous world
there are regular systems of points observable in the
arrangements of atoms and molecules. Crystallography
reveals a good deal about the regularity of point patterns
in nature. A salt crystal can be described as a cubic lattice
with its points occupied alternately by a chlorine atom
and a sodium atom. Each of its lattice points has six
neighbouring points, unlike the diamond which exemplifies
the tetrahedral lattice, or other molecular structures
consisting of several congruent interlocking lattices.
The regularity of pattern is consistent and suggests an
essentially unchanging quality in the points. It might be
asserted that the regularity is possible because of the

one-pointed intelligence within the atom which, clothed in a subtly differentiated aspect of nature, is limited to the expression of this oneness in the guise of a singular and regular pattern. This would answer to the notion of congruence as the intuitive connection of points and to the idea that the One Point contains all potential points and gives meaning to the phenomenal points which then act in the likeness of the original.

In differential geometry it may happen that the curvature of a surface has the same value for all normal sections at a point. When this occurs, the principal directions are said to be indeterminate and the point is referred to as an umbilical point. A surface consisting entirely of umbilical points is also one in which all plane sections are circles composing what we readily recognize as a sphere. In general, the umbilical points of a surface are isolated and the net of lines of curvature may have singular properties at these points only. When the point of a surface assumes all the positions possible on the surface, then the two foci on its normal tend to take on all possible positions on a certain pair of surfaces which are jointly called the evolute or surface of centres of the original surface. In the case of a sphere, the evolute consists of the centre of the sphere alone, since all foci are at this point. Because of this, "the sphere is the only surface for which one sheet of the surface of centres degenerates into a point". Very simply put, a sphere is a "class of points separated from a certain point by a constant distance" and it is also the form which mirrors most perfectly what we intuitively identify as the essential point itself. A surface entirely composed of umbilical points, each of which could become the evolute of myriad generations of spheres, lays the basis for an infinite involution of the principle of the One Point in matter. It can be said that in the universe geometry is integrally embodied in the first view met. Its points are the elementary data of this view and its congruence is the connection of couples of this data. "Then it is embodied again in each one of the following views, successively taking for points and congruence the elementary data of each view and the connection of their couples."

> Infinite love must fill all Eternity as the omnipresence of God and yet it must be infinitely expressed in the smallest moment by enabling one to see in every moment that which is in all. ... It is both ways infinite, for my soul is an infinite sphere at the centre.
>
> THOMAS TRAHERNE

The One Point in space and time is poetically grasped by many sensitive individuals, and yet some, like Dante, have frozen the notion in focussing upon the marvels of a fixed sphere with a central point revealed only at the finish of the journey. This is to look at the idea of the One Point objectively, from the standpoint of the individual pilgrim who is somehow separated from that point in space and time. If one considers the more essential character of the point in itself, it seems to transcend objectivization.

After all, the point has no direction but contains in itself all possible directions. It represents an infinite possibility for action, and in this regard is the perfect symbol of freedom, whilst at the same time remaining a focus of concentration in the midst of the indefinite diffusion of space. "The point wills and wills itself." In space and time there is no fixed point. The moment passes with the circling of the wheel of duration. But the actor can participate in the action of samsara whilst focussing upon a pivotal reality which rests at the centre of the manifest sphere. Metaphysically, it is only because this point exists eternally that all other points are aligned in a circle and there is duration rather than a confused anarchy of moments. Each moment is in relation to others but takes meaning in relation to that which is changeless, eternal and mysteriously outside all others. In this sense it can be said that each moment is in time but also outside of time . . . animated by a non-temporal power.

Leibniz observed that external things present the property of extension to our senses only. This extension of parts takes place in terms of plurality (number), continuity (with time and motion) and coexistence (with non-extended things). Anything continuous is infinitely divisible; there is no end to number, time or motion in this sense. Only that which is truly eternal is neither composite nor has its subsistence in something else. If atoms are divided ad infinitum, they become reduced to mathematical points which would seem to lead to a loss of their extension. Leibniz perceived, however, that their inner life suggested an infinite extension in the metaphysical direction (dimension) where the real essence of what appears in space as a mathematical point can be grasped. In the words of *The Secret Doctrine,* Occultism draws a line between "the absolutely Ideal Universe and the invisible though manifested Kosmos. Our Gods and Monads are not the Elements of extension itself, but only those of the invisible Reality which is the basis of the manifested Kosmos." Thus, every physical point in the universe is but the phenomenal expression of the noumenal Point, whilst the gods and Monads represent unique and ontologically superior expressions of it. Atoms are divisible and extendable, whereas every Monad is a living mirror of the universe. Leibniz said that anything capable of extension must necessarily contain at least two points, an assertion which recognizes that it is not the point itself which is extended.

Plato, following the Pythagorean teachings, frequently referred to cosmology in terms of points (fire), lines (water), superfices (air) and solids (earth). This sequence clearly indicates the conceptual and ontological gap existing between the point and volume, and it lays the basis for understanding how ideation can be expressed in concrete terms. As an aid to this conceptualization, Plato described a point as an extremity of a line, a line as an extremity of a surface, and a surface as an extremity of a solid. Thus the line surpasses a point by one dimension (length), a superfices by two (length and breadth), and a solid by three (length, breadth and depth). These dimensions involve number, which Pythagoras defined as the "extension and energy of the spermatic reasons contained in the Monad". This unity or Monad is the very principle of interval and dimension, but is itself capacious of neither of these conditions. It is the Mother of All Numbers, which the Pythagoreans referred to as Lethe or oblivion, the Rigid Virgin or Atlas who is an ineffable support, connecting and separating all things. They spoke of the Ineffable One of which the Monad is an image and distinguished between it as the cause of all unity and measure, the infinite "cause of all unity and the measure of all things", and the Duad, which is the divisible mother substance.

The point that merges back into the 'circle' after emanating the first three points and connecting them with lines thus forms the first noumenal basis of the Second Triangle in the manifest world. The apex of this triangle is the Monad or Father, the left line the Mother, and the right line the Son. The base line demarcates the universal plane of productive nature and divides the triadic cap in the Pythagorean Decad from the seven points below it. The Pythagoreans saw the monadic apex of this emanation in terms of pure ideation. They attributed scientific knowledge to the duad, opinion to the triad, and sensory perception to the tetrad, thus paralleling the procession of point, line, superfices and solids, which is descriptive of the manifest cosmos. In every such procession the monadic point remains the principle of unchanging unity which determines the relationship of members to each other and to the whole. It is the pivotal point of the Law governing that system, all parts of which behave in a dependent and regular manner. This is because emanation persists during an entire cycle of evolution, and only at the end of that cycle will emanation itself be drawn back into the One Absolute.

In his *De Dignitate,* Pico della Mirandola asserted that man is like a point and a centre to which all parts of the world are related. Man is a point destined to become a circle and to expand is to realize one's potential humanity. In German philosophical thought, from Boehme to Schelling, the entire scheme of life is an unfolding, from a point, of an enveloped God. This they saw as divine expansion and contraction which is mirrored in the procession of human intellection where all interior energy appears in immediate consciousness as a concentrated focus previously disseminated elsewhere in a point. This mental contraction then yields to the broader unity inherent in the more archetypal point by diffusing its energy outward, only to be followed once again by subsequent contraction and expansion. The fundamental image of the autonomy of the mind in consciousness is thus one of a geometric point which eternally formulates and maintains itself. The German philosopher Fichte related the concept of freedom to this image, saying that it "can only be conceived formally as a concentration of the flowing plurality of virtual light on a central point, and as the diffusion of light, from this central point, in a multiplicity that is sustained and lit only in this way". In contemplating the notion of freedom in relation to the One and the many, a progressive transcendence of objectivity is suggested. Seers who are especially trained can conceive of an indivisible unit without slipping into an annihilation of the idea with its subject. They can 'see' the pure dual light of spirit and nature in one.

They see the Real in the unreal, the noetic in the psychic, the noumenal in the phenomenal. In attempting to illustrate this relationship, H.P. Blavatsky wrote, "As a cone stands on its point, or a perpendicular straight line cuts a horizontal plane only in one mathematical point, but may extend infinitely in height and depth, so the essences of things real have only a punctual existence in this physical world of space; but have an infinite depth of inner life in the metaphysical world of thought." This point is one of perfect equilibrium, a zero point or laya state where substance becomes homogeneous and is unable to act or differentiate. Though in a neutral condition to the manifest world, such a point is the Central Spiritual Sun, the ever-emitting life-centre of the cosmos. It is the umbilical point echoed in differential geometry on the phenomenal plane and symbolized in the beautiful myth of Maha Vishnu, from whose navel the lotus containing the universe arose. Floating upon the waters of endless Space, the great Supporter of all the universes contains the ever-concealed Germ capable of emanating forth in a thousand-petalled perfection perceived in every point of time and space by Masters of Wisdom.

This umbilical or zero point is aptly described by the term bindhu, which, whilst simply meaning 'point' or 'spot', also refers to an apparently insignificant incident, the effects of which spread like a drop of oil on water. In the Hindu tradition it is the esoteric term for point, the centre of a mandala and the limit of manifestation. When something exists yet does not exist, it is represented by a bindhu, and at the great dissolution of the universe, all is reabsorbed into the bindhu. In meditation the mind focusses upon the bindhu as the realization of cosmic energy, and when it is worn as a spot on the forehead, it is an affirmation of the role of Shakti. Women entering the *grihastha* stage thus align themselves to the sacred source of creative energy by centering the bindhu spot at the place of the Third Eye.

This spot is a meaningful progeny of the One Point that arose in the immaculate white disk at the dawn of differentiation. Out of this Divine Unity the Ray of the Ever Darkness flashes into the Germ-Point which is matter in the abstract and which ultimately exists in the centre of every subsequent manifest atom. The Circle with one central Point is parentless and numberless. It is Anupadaka and can fall under no calculation. The Point generates the line which represents the Androgynous Logos. When the triad emerges, the Son of the Father fructifies the Virgin matrix of Kosmos, who then gives birth to that form which combines all forms. Thus the progeny of Primordial Light and Chaos is the Central Spiritual Sun, itself a mirror of the Invisible Point from which the Ray was first emitted. According to Hermes Trismegistus, "the point within the circle, was not yet the Architect, but the cause of that Architect; and the latter stood to it in precisely the same relation as the point itself stood to the circumference of the Circle [the immaculate white disk] which cannot be defined". This is what is meant by saying that Parabrahmam cannot be known except through the luminous Point of the Logos which Itself knows only Mulaprakriti, the veil upon Parabrahmam.

This Light of the Logoic Point pervades the universe, and through the Divine Will of the Architects gives birth to every form. From it springs the endless chain of interaction between spirit and matter, giving rise to all chemical action, all molecular structures, all natural forms. The sun is a focus for this on the physical plane, "the lens by which the rays of the primordial Light become materialized", and within every cell of organic life a Monadic synthesis of its essence resides. It is the Germ-Point which is everywhere, the Unmanifest in all manifest forms. Only the focussed concentration of the totally centered human mind is capable of bathing self-consciously in that Light, and to achieve such transcendent one-pointedness requires a deliberate negation of all that is divisible and extended. To make of oneself a zero means to have realized the indivisible, unchanging neutral point within which is the aperture, as it were, opening to the unmanifest potency of the One Eternal Source. At this point the drop may merge with the ocean, the beautiful thousand-petalled lotus with its seed. The world, turning around its still Point, may cease to exist and the vortices of all past and future worlds sigh as they fold in upon themselves in one diminishing bindhu. The Eye of Lord Shiva closes and Maha Vishnu slumbers at one with the Endless Deep. The point is everywhere, without circumference. Everywhere and nowhere, the same.

> *From any point*
> *A line reaches back*
> *And attaches to a far distant centre.*
> *There is no unconnected life in this world,*
> *Nor a point in time*
> *Unknown by any other point.*
> *Nor a tear shed in a vacuum.*

Hermes
July 1981

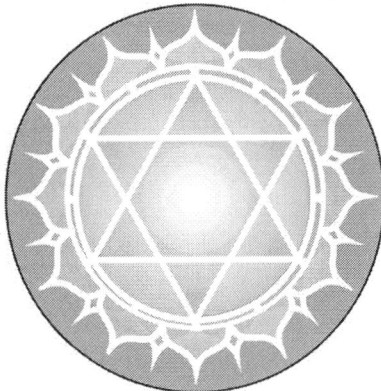

GLOSSARY

Let us use with care those living messengers called words.
W.Q. JUDGE

The Four Immeasurables: A meditative practice prescribed by the Buddha as given in the *Samyuta Nikaya* and common to all schools of Buddhism in which each of the four is directed towards all beings and things (seen or unseen) residing in the six directions of space. In the Pali canon, they are also known as *Brahmā Viharas* — "Divine Abodes of Brahmā, conditions of true *apramāṇa* (unlimited, unbounded mindfulness and vigilance).

1. Maitrī: (Sk., Pali: metta) "friendship", loving-kindness, gentleness and grace. The cultivation of an active interest in the happiness of all beings and things, whether they are perceived as enemies, friends or neither, and whether suffering appears to be present or not.

2. Karuṇā: (Sk.) Compassion, tenderness and mercy, pure universal love and abiding unity with all beings suffering in the six realms of migration.

3. Muditā : Altruistic or sympathetic joy, exhilaration and satisfaction. An impartial, inward rejoicing in the success, welfare and good fortune of others.

4. Upekṣā: Sk. Equanimity, even-mindedness, serenity. A state of inner equipoise and calm continuity that is indifferent to personal gain or loss, honor or dishonor, praise or blame, pleasure or pain.

Monad *(Gr.).* The Unity, the *one;* but in Occultism it often means the unified triad, *Atma-Buddhi-Manas,* or the duad, *Atma-Buddhi,* that immortal part of man which reincarnates in the lower kingdoms, and gradually progresses through them to Man and then to the final goal — Nirvana.

Vivaswat *(Sk.)* The "bright One", the Sun.

Yah *(Heb.).* The word, as claimed in the *Zohar,* through which the Elohim formed the worlds ... one of the many forms of the "Mystery name" IAÔ.

THE GAZE OF THE BUDDHA

It happened that the Holy One and his disciples would come every so often to the five villages between the hills and the river. There in a wide pasture the people gathered to listen.

A villager whose work it was to care for the cows and other animals when they were injured or fell sick had been coming to these gatherings for many years. It could not be said of him that he sought to serve the Buddha, tormented as he knew himself to be by his troubles, with a new child to feed almost every year. But he was glad to join the throng and wonder at the mysterious teachings.

Once, when the monks came into his village to beg for food, he fell into conversation with one of them. He was tending a cow that lay on its side with a broken hoof, lowing piteously. The monk was interested in how he cared for animals. He said that he was from a village to the far north in the mountains which he had left to follow the Buddha. They talked easily together about salves and herbs.

After that whenever the Holy One came, the village veterinarian would look hopefully for this gentle, friendly monk. Often, but not always, they met and would linger together a while, the man parting from the learned monk each time with a lighter heart.

At the open pasture, however, he did not think of approaching any of the disciples. He watched at a distance the Lord and the cluster of yellow robes about him. First one monk would speak, then another ask a question and then another, while the Buddha who spoke more rarely sat a little apart.

Once 'his' monk, sitting off to the side near the Buddha, quietly asked a question. As he went on speaking, the

Buddha turned around in his seat and looked steadily at him.

The villager saw this, as though a window had been thrown open before him, sunlight streaming through, the monk he had grown to love sitting so near the Holy One, the Buddha's gaze of perfect love and trust upon him.

Never after could he forget that moment but neither could he ever quite remember the gaze itself.

CORDELIA SEATON

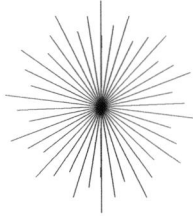

I am extremely dear to the wise man, and he is dear unto me. Excellent indeed are all these, but the spiritually wise is verily myself.
Bhagavad-Gita, Ch.7

OM

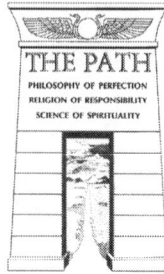

THE PATH
PHILOSOPHY OF PERFECTION
RELIGION OF RESPONSIBILITY
SCIENCE OF SPIRITUALITY

CONCORD GROVE PRESS PUBLICATIONS

Theosophical Tenets
Universal Unity and Causation
Human Solidarity
Karma
Reincarnation
Consciousness and Immortality
Death and Immortality
Civilization: Death and Regeneration
The Language of the Soul
States of Consciousness
Noetic Psychology
Raja Yoga
The Mystery of the Avatar
The Beacon Light
The Service of Humanity
Hit the Mark
The Progress of Humanity
The Ascending Cycle
The Religion of Solidarity
The Dream of Ravan

The Jewel in the Lotus
The Gates of Gold
The Voice of the Silence
The Dhammapada
The Bhagavad Gita
The Doctrine of the Bhagavad Gita
The Law of Sacrifice
The Grihastha Ashrama
Novus Ordo Seclorum
Parapolitics—Toward the City of Man
The Moral and Political Thought of Mahatma Gandhi
The Law of Violence and the Law of Love
The Society of the Future
Utilitarianism and All That
The Platonic Quest
The Banquet
Objectivity and Consciousness

SECRET DOCTRINE SERIES

Presenting selected passages from *The Secret Doctrine* by Helena Petrovna Blavatsky, each pamphlet in the series focuses upon a key theme for study and reflection.

The Gupta Vidya
The Book of Dzyan
Glyphs and Symbols
Gods, Monads & Atoms
The Great Sacrifice
Globes, Rounds & Races

Space
Duration
Motion
The Logos
Cosmic Hierarchies
Cyclic Evolution

Meta-Geometry
Meta-Astronomy
Meta-Biology
Meta-Psychology
Meta-Chemistry
Meta-Geology

1407 Chapala Street, Santa Barbara, California 93101
www.concordgrovepress.org

Made in the USA
Las Vegas, NV
13 July 2024